OUR BODIES
Male & Female

written by
D.M. Brock & **Monica Ashour**

designed by
David Fiegenschue & **Emily Gudde**

Level 7
BOOK 1
Second Edition

Dedicated to the Church, including our family and friends, and especially to Mother Mary and Saint John Paul.

Tremendous thanks to all TOBET members over the years. Special thanks to Alyssan, Amy, Andrea, Chris, DeAnn, Erika, Jonathan, Kathy, Luke, Joe, Patrick, Sheryl, and Véronique. Special thanks for Fr. John Bayer, O.C. We are grateful for consultation work by the translator of the *Theology of the Body*, Dr. Michael Waldstein, as well as Dr. Susan Waldstein. We are also grateful for the consultation work of Katrina J. Zeno, MTS.

Nihil Obstat: Tomas Fuerte, S.T.L.
Censor Librorum

Imprimatur: +Most Reverend Samuel J. Aquila, S.T.L.
Archbishop of Denver
Denver, Colorado, USA
Feast of Saints Joachim and Ann • July 28, 2020

Library of Congress information on file. ISBN 978-1-945845-36-9 • Second Edition

Cover Design: FigDesign • Layout: Emily Gudde • Editor: Dayspring Brock • Associate Editor: Alexis Mausolf

Excerpts from the English translation of the *Catechism of the Catholic Church*. New York: Catholic Book Publishing Co., 1994. Based on John Paul II's *Man and Woman He Created Them: A Theology of the Body*. Trans. Michael Waldstein, Copyright © 2006. Used by permission of Pauline Books & Media, 50 Saint Paul's Ave, Boston, Massachusetts 02130. All rights reserved. www.pauline.org. All Scripture verses are from the *New American Bible*, Revised Edition (NABRE). Excerpts from YOUCAT. Trans. Michael J. Miller (San Francisco: Ignatius Press, 2011) www.ignatius.com. Used with permission. The subtitles on page 12 and some concepts on p.13 are based on *Chance or the Dance: A Critique of Modern Secularism*. T. Howard. (San Francisco: Ignatius Press, 2018) www.ignatiuspress.com. Used with permission. The quote on p.12 and concept on pgs. 13 and 24 are based on *The Theology of the Liturgy: The Sacramental Foundation of Christian Existence*. Joseph Ratzinger. (San Francisco: Ignatius Press, 2014) www.ignatius.com. Used with permission. The paraphrase on p. 16 is from John Paul II. "On the Dignity and Vocation of Women." *The Holy See*. Rome, August 15, 1988, w2.vatican.va/content/john-paul-ii/en/apost_letters/1988/documents/hf_jp-ii_apl_19880815_mulieris-dignitatem.html. The statistic on p.18 is from the University of Utah. "Why males pack a powerful punch: Upper arm strength, different from females." *Science Daily*, 5 February 2020. www.sciencedaily.com/releases/2020/02/200205132404.htm. Public domain. The quote on p. 28 is from John Paul II. "Letter to Women for Beijing Conference." *The Holy See*. Rome, June 29, 1995, w2.vatican.va/content/john-paul-ii/en/letters/1995/documents/hf_jp-ii_let_29061995_women.html. *Justice League* & all associated names, *The Lord of the Rings* & all associated names, *Star Wars* and all associated names, and *The Avengers* are property of their respective owners and all of these are used for educational purposes only.

Image Credits: Shutterstock: pg 5 ©Studio Lucky / pg 6 ©testing / pg 16 ©fizkes / pg 17 ©Monkey Business Images / pg 18 ©Blazej Lyjak / pg 19 ©PR Image Factory / pg 22 ©OHishiapply (left) ©Everett Collection (top left) / pg 23 ©Tinseltown (top right) ©Kathy Hutchins (bottom right) / pg 27 ©lassedesignen / pg 29 ©Christo / pg 32 ©zulufoto / pg 33 ©George Rudy / pg 34 ©FXQuadro (left & right) / pg 38 © fizkes / pg 40 ©wavebreakmedia / pg 45 ©Antonio Guillem (left) ©Anna Om (right) / pg 47 ©Kamira /// Getty Images: pg 15 Tim Graham (left) / pg 6 ©testing / pg 22 ©Universal History Archive (bottom left) ©Pictorial Parade (bottom right) ©Apic (right) / pg 23 ©Allan Grant (left) ©Universal History Archive (top left) ©The Asahi Shimbun (right) / pg 28 ©Authenticated News /// Other: pg 15 ©Lake City CW (right). Used with permission. / pg 22 no author, public domain (top right) commons.wikimedia.org/wiki/File:santa_laura.jpg / pg 23 ©Associazione Pier Giorgio Frassati, Rome. Used with permission. / pg 31 ©Erin Barcevac. Used with permission.

Printed in the United States of America. © Copyright 2021 Monica Ashour. All rights reserved. No part of this book may be reproduced or transmitted in any form or by any means, electronic or mechanical, including photocopying, recording, or by any information storage and retrieval system without permission in writing from the publisher.

Table of Contents

1 — **Created to Complement** — 4
- God designed the two sexes to complement each other.
- Stereotypes distort truth, but archetypes reveal truth.
- Family life teaches what it means to be male and female.

2 — **The Mystery of Femininity & Masculinity** — 12
- The visible world reveals invisible realities.
- Both women and men are able to connect and protect.
- Each person has individual gifts to be shared with others.

3 — **Masculine and Feminine Archetypes** — 26
- The mark of a heroine or hero is excellence of soul.
- Archetypes are universal patterns that have been imprinted in our hearts.
- As archetypes show us, heroic women and men sacrifice for the good of others.

4 — **Attraction and Love** — 36
- Evaluating attractions is a sign of maturity.
- Self-mastery is good preparation for relationships.
- Objects are for use; persons are for love.

1 Created to Complement

Boy or Girl?

When a baby is born, what is the first question everyone asks? Is it, "What color are the eyes?" "How many toes?" or "What does the belly button look like?" Of course not! The child's sex—whether male or female—is what everyone is eager to know. Parents often like to find out their baby's sex ahead of time through an ultrasound.

What is it about being male or female that intrigues and delights us so much? We know that both males and females have arms, legs, faces, fingers, and toes. But it is their differences that fascinate us.

Is our baby a boy or a girl?

- What should we name our baby?
- Will our baby look like me or my husband?
- What will our baby's talents be?
- What will our baby's personality be like?

© Copyright 2018 by Monica Ashour. All rights reserved.

Beyond Plain Vanilla

Imagine life with no differences. What if every person were alike in age, height, and skin color? We would be a uniform species, with little to learn from one another. And if this logic were applied to the rest of the world, there would be no delicious array of ice creams, no colorful variety of birds to fill the skies, and no startling assortment of underwater creatures inhabiting the ocean depths.

Fortunately, life is full of variety. The world boasts of more than 8 million different species! And if we zero in on just our own species, we realize that each human body is unique and unrepeatable. What does this tell us? The variety in creation reveals something about the Creator.

God loves an assortment of colors, flavors, smells, textures, sights, and sounds. He doesn't settle for just plain vanilla. Indeed, creation finds profound meaning in contrast. Think of it like this: the experience of a thing is further illuminated when contrasted to another thing. For example, introverts and extroverts bring each other different perspectives.

The arts and the sciences challenge one another, and even in nature, the contrast of winter and summer increases our appreciation of each. This is called a **complementary** relationship. Like colors on contrasting sides of the color wheel, there is beauty in the difference.

"God created mankind in his image, in the image of God he created them; male and female he created them." *Gen. 1:27*

The Skill of the Skate

Complementary relationships are most apparent in humanity—in the two sexes, male and female. The word *sex* comes from a Latin word meaning "to divide or separate." This shows that humanity is divided naturally into two groups, male or female.

The two sexes experience the world uniquely, and each deepens the perspective of the other. Women and men complement each other; they go together well.

Have you ever watched a pair of figure-skaters? There is a male skater and a female skater. Both must be physically strong and artistically graceful, but it is the male skater who always does the lifts and throws, and it is the female skater who can fly and spin with grace. The cooperation of the two sexes is moving and elegant. His strength and skill are at the service of her beauty and finesse. They complement each other by their differences.

The First Human—Adam

Think back to the creation story; here we see how complementarity and love interact. Adam realized that there was no**body** like him—no other human. He desired a companion. He needed someone **like** him yet someone **unlike** him in order to give the total gift of himself.

God's Creation of Eve

The creation of Eve was a gift both to Eve and to Adam. Eve was like Adam, a human person, both body and spirit—but different—female. Now Adam and Eve were able to give the total gift of self to each other as husband and wife.

Interestingly, God fashioned Eve from Adam's rib—not from his head and not from his foot. The fact that God brought her forth from Adam's side shows that women and men are equal, meant to walk side by side through life.

Openness to Life

God created Adam and Eve to be fruitful and multiply (see Gen. 1:28). The ability to procreate—to have children—is a sign of the complementarity of man and woman. We all have received the gift of life thanks to both sexes.

The Meaning of Adam's Rib

Scripture Shows	Theology of the Body Translates
The rib is taken from Adam's side, not from his head or foot.	Woman and man are equal in dignity.
The rib is taken from Adam's (human) body.	Woman and man belong to each other, sharing the same (human) nature.
The rib is taken from a place that covers the heart.	Woman and man are to protect each other's hearts.

Based on John Paul II's footnote 15 (*TOB* 8:4). © Copyright 2018 by Monica Ashour. All rights reserved.

Stereotypes

In our present age, there's a lot of confusion about what it means to be male or female, but much of this confusion is due to stereotypes. A stereotype is an oversimplified idea about a group of people. Have you ever walked through the baby clothes section in a department store and wondered, "Who assigned pink to girls and blue to boys?" Sometimes, society can assign superficial qualities, or stereotypes, to masculinity and femininity.

Stereotypes can lead to anger and misunderstanding. Consider this make-believe stereotype: short people are nicer than tall people. You might respond, "That's not true! I know lots of nice tall people!"

Stereotypes distort truth. We all recognize this clearly in middle school, where people are stereotyped by labels like nerd, jock, overachiever, loner, etc. Why are these labels unfair? Stereotypes can box us in, not allowing us the freedom to grow in understanding our true selves. We desire the same freedom when considering the differences between men and women.

Do all guys have to play sports? Must all girls love shopping? Some stereotypes are based on a kernel of truth that comes from observing particular traits seen in a majority of people. However, our identities as male or female run much deeper than these. There is mystery in being made male or female. And mysteries gradually reveal truth to us, layer by layer.

Archetypes

Rather than stereotypes, let's look to archetypes [ARK-ə-types]. An archetype is an original pattern revealing a universal truth. Archetypes show the essence of a thing. Take the archetypes of Fatherhood and Motherhood. The terms "Father-Sky" and "Mother-Earth" refer to these universal archetypes. The sky "fathers" by sending forth rain to the earth, and in turn, the earth "mothers" by receiving and bringing forth fruit. To try to say "Mother-Sky" and "Father-Earth" doesn't take archetypes seriously, for a father, like the sky, gives of himself, and a mother, like the earth, receives and then bears new life.

While it is wise to reject outdated or inaccurate stereotypes, we should not reject archetypes. Archetypes **reveal** truth while stereotypes **distort** truth.

Look at some common archetypes below. You would never say that Alice in Wonderland symbolizes what it means to be a villain, nor that Darth Vader represents what it means to be innocent. Archetypes are not interchangeable. They are universally recognized symbols that point to the nature of a thing.

Common Archetypes

Archetype	Description	Examples
Everyman	regular person journeying through life	Alice in Wonderland, Frodo, Meg Murry
Innocent	dreamer, pure, wholesome	Samwise Gamgee, The Little Prince, Snow White
Hero	dragon slayer, soldier, crusader	Spiderman, Wonder Woman, Superman
Villain	betrayer, vengeful, evil-doer	The Joker, White Witch of Narnia, Darth Vader

© Copyright 2018 by Monica Ashour. All rights reserved.

The Family Archetypes

Male and female archetypes are best taught through family relationships. Males are **sons**, **brothers**, **husbands**, and **fathers**. Females are **daughters**, **sisters**, **wives**, and **mothers**. Each member of the family complements the others. We will cover most of these archetypes later in the book, but now let's look briefly at the archetypes of son and daughter. They teach us about masculinity and femininity and are crucial to understanding our relationship to God.

Sons and Daughters

As a son or daughter, from the very first moment of existence, you received many traits from your parents. You may have received the color of your dad's eyes or his dry sense of humor, your mom's smile or her mathematical skills. Your genetic attributes and your abilities are an important part of identity, but they don't tell the whole story.

Your deepest identity is as a son or daughter of God the Father. When you are baptized, you receive divine life and are adopted into God's family. God the Father gives to you His love, mercy, and grace. And you, as His daughter or son, receive these divine gifts. In fact, your very life is a gift to be received from God Who knows you personally.

"As proof that you are children, God sent the spirit of his Son into our hearts, crying out, 'Abba, Father!'" *Gal. 4:6*

"...[M]asculinity and femininity [are] two different 'incarnations,' that is, two ways [of being human]."   *Theology of the Body 8:1*

The Body as Answer Key

God also gives you the gift of your body to help you understand your identity. Have you ever worked out a math problem and then checked the answer key in the back of the book to find that you got it wrong? Thank goodness for the answer key! It helps you figure out where you got off track. The body is like an answer key that allows us to compare our feelings with God's design. What does the "answer key" of your body say?

First, your body teaches that you are a human being. Secondly, your body teaches that you are either male or female. If a doctor took a swab of your inside cheek, the results would identify you as male or female because every one of your cells has either XX chromosomes (female) or XY chromosomes (male). Your DNA informs you of your sex. That means the body clearly teaches your identity as male or female.

Points to Ponder:
1. What woman is a good role model of femininity in your life? What man is a good role model of masculinity in your life? Why?
2. As a class, discuss the stereotype and then the archetype for the following: scientist, princess, police officer, librarian, athlete, etc.

Mission: Girls, you will always be God the Father's beloved daughter. Boys, you will always be God the Father's beloved son. At Mass, picture Jesus giving His very self on the Cross to you personally. He knew you then; He knows you now.

2 The Mystery of Femininity and Masculinity

Chance...

Let's delve deeper into the meaning of humanity. Ask yourself, "What does it mean to be a human person?" There are some who believe that persons are good only if they are useful. This is a functionalistic attitude that says all matter can be manipulated according to people's desires. It explains human history, culture, and behavior only in terms of usefulness, and claims that all of life exists only by chance.

The "chance" theory leaves no room for mystery or meaning in human life. For example, love might be defined as mere chemical reactions. Moreover, if "chance" were true, then there would be no motivation to be good or to do good: Why not pollute the Earth? Why not be disrespectful to your teacher, and treat members of the other sex as objects? When things or persons lose meaning, they are not shown proper reverence.

...or the Dance?

Contrary to the "chance" theory, Christianity knows that the material world is imbued with supernatural realities that give meaning to life. Christianity respects matter, meaning, and mystery. Christians view life as a cosmic dance: divine music plays for us all, and each person has special steps to perform so that together, we create something beautiful.

In other words, human life is a gift and our biological realities have deep significance. A smile is more than a biological reality; it is a sign of gladness. Singing is more than a biological reality; it points to human emotion and creativity. We live in a world infused with meaning. We were born for the dance.

> "[Through] the 'transparency' of the biological, [persons] can glimpse the spiritual and eternal."
> —Joseph Ratzinger, *Liturgy*, 158

The Catholic View

With His Incarnation, Jesus showed us that matter is good and that persons are gifts. As Catholics, we know that God reveals mysteries to us through the material world. This is called having a "sacramental view" of reality.

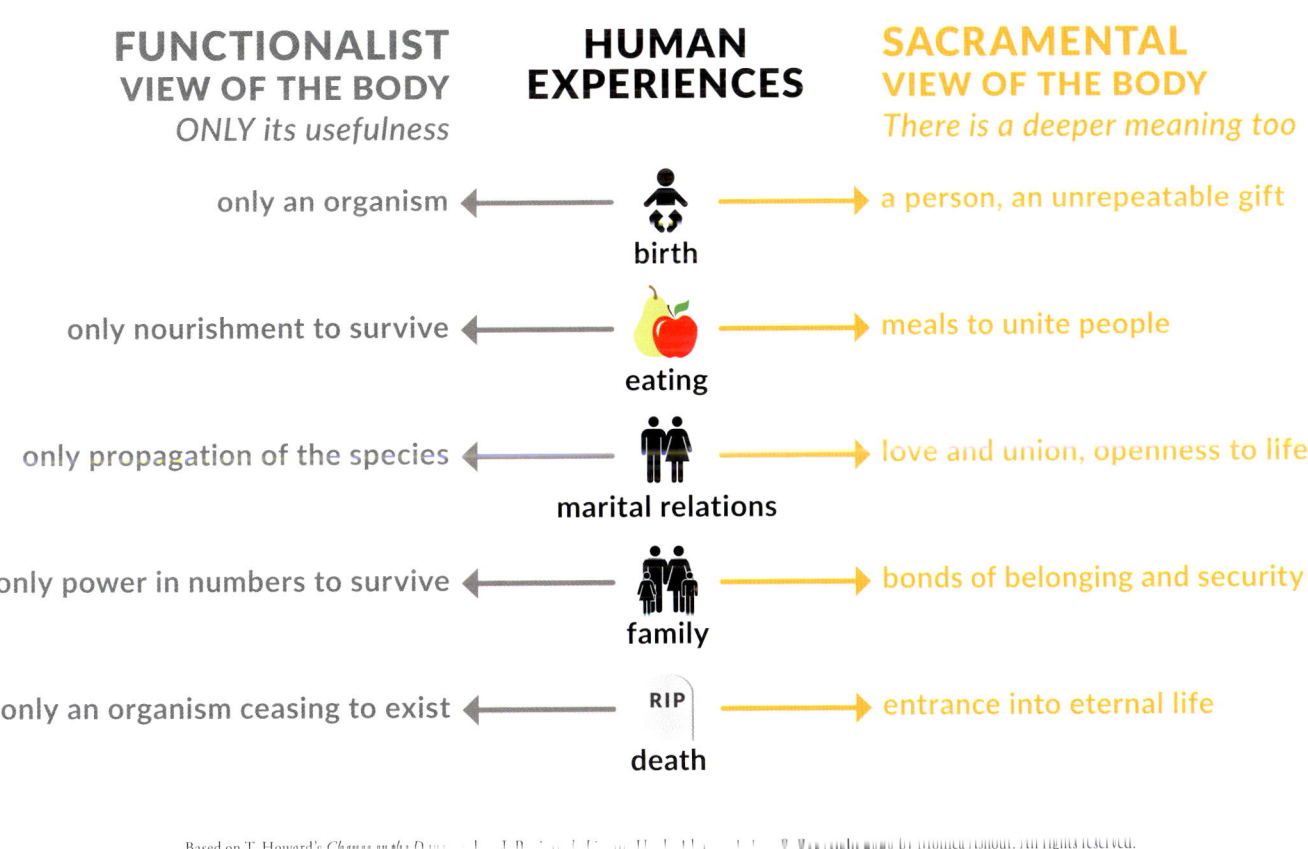

The Quest toward Mystery

Knowing we are born for the dance means that there is a spiritual reality to all of creation and especially the human body. Therefore, the distinction between males and females carries a God-given meaning.

God's design of the woman's body reflects the internal and the relational, from her rich emotional life and her inner strength, to her receptive organs that permit the hidden gestation of a child. It is true that not every woman has children, but every woman is called to be a "spiritual mother" insofar as she makes a gift of self for life and love.

A woman is inclined toward what is personal and concrete. Women devote their whole being to others through careers, projects, and the families entrusted to them. This is why God the Father entrusted Jesus to a woman, Mary. As the archetype of femininity, Mary changed the course of history.

God's design of the man's body reflects the external and the physical, from his muscular structure to his testosterone levels that permit strenuous activity, whether as a construction worker, as a scholar, or as a father.

It is true that not every man is called to father a child, but every man is created to be a "spiritual father" insofar as he makes a gift of self for life and love.

A man brings a special kind of sacrificial spirit to his family, job, and community. His gifts include enduring hardships and persevering for the sake of others. This is why God the Father asked His Son, Jesus, to save all of us. As the archetype of masculinity, Jesus Christ changed the course of history.

Does this mean that men are not devoted to others or that women do not sacrifice? Of course not! However, male and female bodies reveal aspects of their unique gifts of self. Men and women are not interchangeable pieces in the great puzzle of life.

Both man and woman are created in God's image and likeness, and each reflects different qualities of the Creator. Moveover, when a husband and wife form a reciprocal communion of persons, they more perfectly image the Triune God, Who is the first communion of Persons.

Heroic Femininity

In October 1985, the United Nations Secretary General, Javier Pérez de Cuéllar, called St. Teresa of Calcutta the "most powerful woman in the world." Paradoxically, it was her simplicity and love that were so powerful. As a religious sister from Albania assigned to teach in India, Mother Teresa heard a call from God to serve the poorest of the poor, by offering them life and love. This small woman of great faith started ministering to those dying on the streets. A few sisters joined her, and she eventually founded the Missionaries of Charity, which is now a worldwide congregation that ministers sacrificially to thousands upon thousands of those most in need. No wonder she is called "Mother."

Heroic Masculinity

Blessed Franz Jägerstätter was an Austrian farmer and family man who refused to fight for or swear allegiance to Hitler after he was drafted by the Nazis. He valued his conscience and fidelity to God more than he did earthly life and security. A devoted husband and father, he knew that guiding and protecting his family entailed martyrdom. Yet, his strong faith gave him courage to face death, holding fast to the assurance that he and his family would be reunited one day in Heaven. The night before being executed by the Nazis, Franz wrote, "Neither prison nor chains nor sentence of death can rob a man of the Faith and his free will. God gives so much strength that it is possible to bear any suffering...."

Feminine Connecting

As we have learned, the male body and the female body point beyond themselves to the truth of masculinity and femininity, respectively. To further explore what the masculine and feminine are, let's focus on two significant characteristics that God gives to all human persons: connecting and protecting.

Notice how these two qualities complement each other. Connecting brings people together in friendship and communion. Protecting provides limits and boundaries for safety. To whom has God given the greater responsibility for bringing people together? Who usually excels at connecting? Women. St. John Paul II says that women "see with the heart." Both scientific observation and conventional wisdom agree that women are naturally gifted with emotional intelligence.

God gives everyone the gift of emotions in order to allow us to experience life fully, though we are not meant to be mastered by runaway passions or impulses. Yet, in "On the Dignity and Vocation of Women," St. John Paul says that sensitivity is a specific characteristic of femininity.

Feminine sensitivity responds to the need for all persons to connect—physically, emotionally, and spiritually—whether in a friendship, family, or community. Women also bring to society the indispensable gift of uniting reason and feeling, thus emphasizing the "personal" dimension in the workplace.

Masculine Connecting

Although females may have a more natural gift for relationships, all persons need connection. It is a false stereotype to believe that if a boy is emotionally expressive, that makes him feminine. A man who learns how to be nurturing is not less masculine, but more masculine, for he is more himself—a human person who thrives in committed, connected relationships.

How do males connect? A man reaches out to others through sports, work, conversation, humor, play, and advice. By being emotionally present, he establishes trust and stability. He is naturally drawn toward interpersonal communion, but expresses it in a masculine way. St. John Paul II teaches that a man is meant to provide tenderness for his wife and children. By connecting, he protects them from self-doubt, loneliness, and hopelessness.

"The 'affirmation of the person' is nothing other than welcoming the gift...."
Theology of the Body 15:4

Masculine Protecting

Connecting is complemented by protecting. Whereas women are naturally adept at connecting, men have particular gifts for protecting, since men are generally more physically powerful.

As the *Science Daily* observes: "It's already known that males' upper bodies, on average, have 75% more muscle mass and 90% more strength than females."* Why? Think back to prehistoric times when people lived in caves or tents. Who would protect the family or tribe against wild animals, the elements, and enemies? The man. His muscular build allowed him to stand between his loved ones and any danger.

God gives strength to every person to protect and serve others. Yet, one of the most evident God-given callings for men is strength in the service of love. Strength is a gift, as long as it is not used to dominate or bully other people.

A man who has both inner and outer strength will not intimidate his family, but will seek to support their physical, emotional, and spiritual needs.

Science Daily, 5 February 2020. www.sciencedaily.com

"Husbands, love your wives, even as Christ loved the church and handed himself over for her...." Eph. 5:25

"The presence of the feminine element, next to the masculine and together with it, signifies an enrichment for [humanity] in the whole perspective of... history, including the history of salvation."
Theology of the Body 10:1

Feminine Protecting

While protecting may be easier for males, all persons need to learn to protect. It is a false stereotype to assume that if a woman is protective or strong, she must be masculine. In fact, a woman who has learned to protect is more feminine, for she is more herself—a person who looks out for others and is willing to sacrifice herself for their sake.

Have you ever heard the term "Mama Bear"? It describes a woman who fights tooth and nail to protect her children. A woman's physical strength and emotional intelligence work together for the well-being of the family. Think about a mom who protects the hearts of her husband and children. By listening to their fears, hurts, joys, and questions, she also protects by connecting.

Men and women who respect the gifts of the other sex and learn to incorporate them in their own lives are actually more complete, more well-rounded, and more inspiring persons. Their gifts of self complement each other and enrich the whole of society.

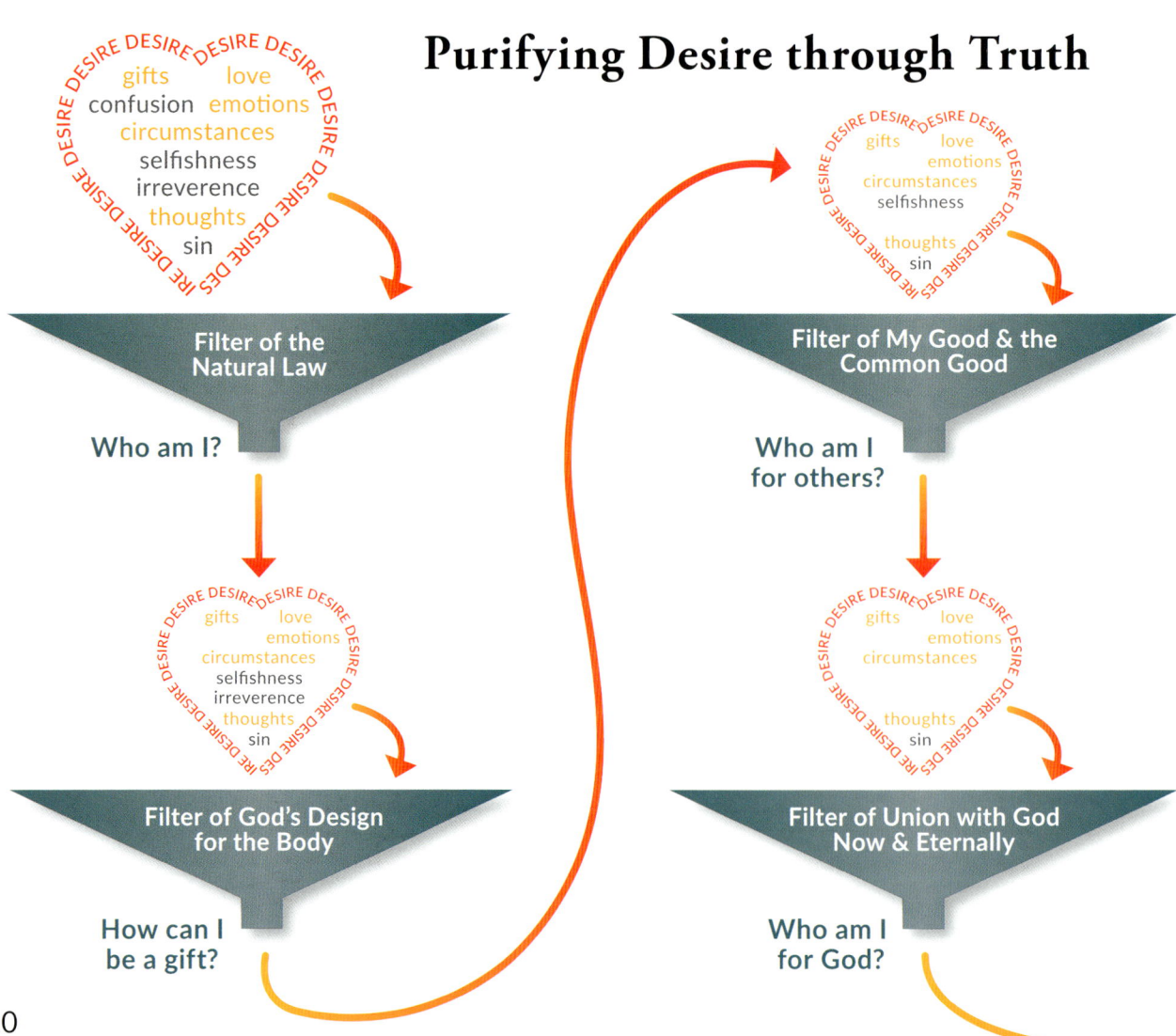

Theology of the Body: The Best Gender Study

In a world that seeks to deny the essence of man and of woman and claims that gender is whatever you feel at the moment, it is important to evaluate your feelings using Revelation and Natural Law, which includes reason and science. You can then sift out any falsehoods you may have absorbed from the culture or from fallen human nature. The more you purify your desires, the more freedom you gain to become your authentic self. As you do so, keep these standards in mind:

1. Your identity is found in the Natural Law.
2. Your body matters and deserves reverence.
3. You are made as a gift to be a gift for others.
4. Your ultimate destiny and desire are to be with God and others in Heaven.

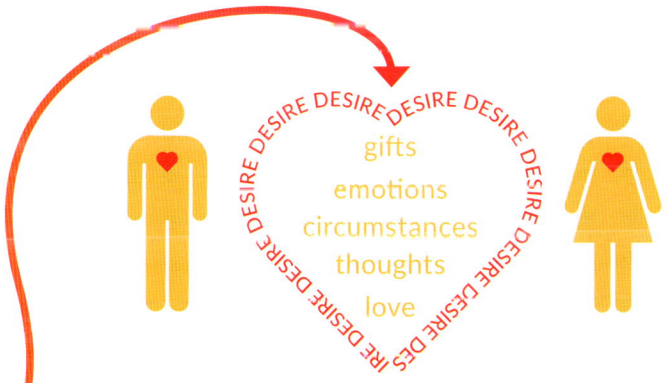

My real self—healthy, joyful, and free to thrive

Consider this: Did you know that a few decades ago, people thought that only men should be astronauts? Why? Would a woman have to deny her body and her femininity to become an astronaut? Not at all. That cultural stereotype was wrong. A girl who knows that she is gifted in aerospace engineering can help others and serve God by becoming an astronaut. Aeronautics is a worthwhile pursuit and does not require that a woman deny the truth of her body. She is free to become an astronaut.

What about this scenario? Can a boy who knows he is very good at babysitting decide to give birth someday? No! As a male, he must take into account the built-in structure of his body. But what if he decided to become a kindergarten teacher? Yes, he is free to make that choice; being a kindergarten teacher is a noble pursuit and does not contradict the truth of his body.

Right now, you may not know what you want to be when you grow up. Your task is to purify your desires through truth and be aware of your gifts and talents. In this way, your mission will gradually be unveiled to you. Only you can give your unique gift for the good of the world.

21

Free to Thrive

As long as we accept the God-given design of our bodies as a gift, there are countless ways to live out our own unique identities for the common good. Each person's mission is to give the gift of self, in big or small ways.

Marie Curie

Polish-French physicist, discovered new elements & won two Nobel prizes

Laura Montoya

Colombian religious sister, founded the Order of St. Catherine of Siena

Tamarine Tanasugarn

Thai professional tennis player

Flannery O'Connor

American author, won three "O. Henry Awards" for short fiction

Harriet Tubman

African American military scout & spy, freed slaves, and fought for women's rights

Grace Kelly

American Hollywood star & Princess of Monaco

FREE TO GIVE LIFE & LOVE

A woman carries out her mission in her own uniquely feminine way, a man in his own uniquely masculine way. Can you describe how the people pictured on these pages exhibit both connecting and protecting?

Gregor Mendel

Austrian priest, founder of the modern science of genetics

Augustine Tolton

First Black American priest, ex-slave, and devoted pastor

Jackie Robinson

Hall of Famer, first African American to play Major League Baseball

José Sánchez del Río

14-year-old Mexican martyr, executed for not renouncing his faith

Pier Giorgio Frassati

Italian mountain climber & Catholic social activist

Eduardo Verástegui

Mexican actor & producer, pro-life founder of Manto de Guadalupe

FREE TO GIVE LIFE & LOVE

The Goal of Our Quest

Seeing Men and Women Sacramentally

Throughout our lives, God gradually reveals His plan of self-giving love. He gives His extravagant Gift of Self to us sacramentally in His Body and Blood. We, as persons made in God's image, are also created to give the gift of self. This we know because of the design of the male body and female body; they are alike yet complementary, gifts to each other. On your quest called life, ask yourself: "What is my mission?" and "How can I love God and others authentically?" and "How does the goal of Heaven help me to find my real self?" and "How can I learn to entrust myself to my loving Father Who calls me to be a gift?"

The Mystery of Masculinity and Femininity

God created two "incarnational" ways to love—femininity and masculinity—which open themselves up to "an-other." Human love in the divine plan is an image of God's very own inner life. God is not a single person who demands servile obedience, but three self-giving Persons, united in love. The mystery of masculinity and femininity, seen sacramentally, shows forth Trinitarian Love itself. How important, then, it is to see femininity and masculinity properly, not as outworn stereotypes, but as archetypes of universal truths. There we pause, showing reverence for the mystery, the mystery of life and love.

Points to Ponder:
1. Name two ways that a Catholic sacramental view of masculinity and femininity (see pages 20–21 & 24) is different than some of the cultural messages.
2. What are some practical ways to start living as a hero or heroine? Since we are made to be great, how can you aspire to greatness in everyday life?

Mission: Look for various expressions of "the dance" around you and ponder their deeper meaning. (Ex: You have new neighbors; that may mean God is providing new friends. You were disciplined by your teacher; maybe God is saying it is time to grow in maturity. You had a lot of fun with friends; maybe God is showing you that being with and for others brings joy.)

3 Masculine and Feminine Archetypes

The Archetypes of Hero and Heroine

Having defeated Doomsday, Superman is infected with a virus that causes mutations within him, including an "inner beast" that seeks to get out and destroy others. His friend Wonder Woman knows he is not himself, and so she flies him to outer space, away from the kryptonite which was doing him further harm. Finally returning to himself, Superman, along with Wonder Woman and the rest of the Justice League, defeats the evil Brainiac.

Why do so many people love the *Justice League*, *The Avengers*, and the heroes of *The Lord of the Rings*? Fairy tales, legends, myths, and folklore affect us the same way, inspiring us all and coloring our imaginations. What makes these stories so appealing is that they are filled with archetypes, especially the archetype of the male hero and the female heroine.

Recall that archetypes are universal patterns that have been imprinted in human culture since the beginning of time. (The word *archetype* comes from *arche*—"beginning"—and *type*—"imprint".) Our need for the timeless truth of archetypes never wanes.

In Greek mythology, the mark of the heroine or hero is *arete*, or "excellence of soul". We admire heroines and heroes not only because they rigorously follow a demanding set of rules, but also because they dedicate themselves unwaveringly and self-sacrificially to a mission grounded in truth. Committed to the good, they undertake difficult tasks and eventually defeat evil. The archetypes of heroic women and men display virtues such as integrity, strength, discipline, wisdom, courage in suffering, and a concern for the common good.

Girls as Heroines; Boys as Heroes

Let's consider a few of these universal qualities of the heroine or hero in two familiar stories. Take, for example, Galadriel in *The Lord of the Rings*. At one point, Frodo offers Galadriel the Ring of Power. She understands immediately that this ring would give her immense power and protection for her people, but at the expense of her own honor and nobility. Although sorely tempted, she remains focused on what is truly good and declines the Ring, defeating its deceptive allure of evil power. She is a true heroine, an embodiment of virtue. She illustrates how all of us can actually rise above temptation and adversity.

What about the archetype of hero in *Star Wars*? Luke Skywalker learns discipline and undivided focus from Obi Wan Kenobi and Yoda, who teach him what it means to be a courageous Jedi Knight, dedicated to the common good. Despite discovering that his father is the evil Darth Vader ("Dark Father"), he clings to his stronger identity as a Jedi Knight and fights bravely for the survival of his people. An archetype for all of us, Luke Skywalker overcomes evil, both internally and externally.

Although these examples are fictional, they represent universal human experiences. Can you identify with these heroes? The experiences of Galadriel and Luke Skywalker mirror our own heritage of Original Sin, and they challenge each of us to turn away from evil and find our deeper identities in God, Who is Absolute Goodness. He is trustworthy and desires our good.

27

The Sister as Heroine

Sophie Scholl and her brother Hans were German teenagers in the 1930s when the Nazis, led by Hitler, began persecuting the Jews. In resistance, Sophie and Hans formed a secret society called "The White Rose." Sophie threw herself into the work, helping to create pamphlets that opposed the racist Nazi ideology. She and Hans were eventually caught by the Gestapo, sent to prison, and condemned in an unfair trial. Sophie, a heroic sister, and her brother were both executed for their convictions.

Sophie's compassion for the suffering of others gave her the courage to face an evil empire and mortal danger. Girls, you may not be called to extreme action like Sophie, but you can radiate Christ and be heroic sisters to all when you:
- Bring your heroic femininity and freedom to the world by exploring, creating, and achieving.
- Create connections and express compassion.
- Welcome others with hospitality, even when it requires sacrifice and effort.
- Risk being made fun of, as you go against prevailing attitudes for the sake of doing good.
- Grow in the sisterhood of female friendships, like the Virgin Mary and Elizabeth in the Bible.

Sophie Scholl and Hans Scholl, sister and brother

"Thank you, *women who are daughters and women who are sisters*! Into the heart of the family, and then of all society, you bring the richness of your sensitivity, your intuitiveness, your generosity and fidelity."
—St. John Paul II,
Letter to Women

The Brother as Hero

27-year-old Fernando and his younger sister, Rosie, were just leaving a Dallas restaurant, when two men started to harass Rosie. Fernando told them to leave her alone, but as he and his sister walked away, the men followed them. Fernando turned around and fought off the two men, who turned out to be members of a gang. As revenge, the gang members found out where Fernando lived, and a few days later, they killed him.

Fernando defended Rosie's honor and paid for it with his life. His actions show how men protect through their heroic, masculine gift of self. Boys, you may not be asked to offer the ultimate sacrifice like Fernando, but you can imitate Christ and be heroic brothers to all when you:
- Bring your heroic masculinity and freedom to the world by achieving, learning, and creating an atmosphere of goodwill.
- Practice courtesy by offering your seat, opening a door, or carrying things for others.
- Stand up for younger children and for any victim of bullying.
- Show self-mastery by not participating in degrading "locker-room" talk.
- Grow in the brotherhood of male friendships, like David and Jonathan in the Bible.

As a Christian, you can grow in maturity by seeing each person as a brother or sister in Christ. Practice heroic virtue. Boys, live out the truth of your masculinity as a brother to all. Girls, live out the truth of your femininity as a sister to all.

"A virtue is an interior disposition, a positive habit, a passion that has been placed at the service of the good."
YOUCAT 299

The Wife as Heroine

Brigid, a non-practicing Catholic, and Kurt, a non-practicing Lutheran, were in love and engaged to be married, but Brigid faced an inner struggle. She felt God calling her back to the Catholic Church. She feared Kurt would shun her, but she knew she needed to be obedient to God's will. Though puzzled by her spiritual conversion, Kurt supported her. After their wedding, Brigid continued to journey toward God, asking Him to touch Kurt's heart. Fourteen years later, Brigid and their children rejoiced as Kurt became Catholic at the Easter Vigil.

Brigid's heroic fidelity to God included a risk: losing Kurt. A strong wife knows how to navigate between two extremes: the side that says a woman finds her identity **only** in relationship to a man; and the side that says a woman is utterly self-sufficient and needs no one, especially not a man. The first approach to femininity says a woman's self-worth depends on being "in a relationship." The other extreme forgets that God made persons **for** each other.

St. John Paul II bridges this divide. He reminds us that authentic femininity is industrious, takes initiative, and is deeply relational. The heroic wife believes in her husband and brings out the best in him, even when he may doubt himself. She harmonizes her value as a person with devotion to her husband. A holy wife knows that her central task is to help her husband draw closer to Christ.

For or Against?

Husband **and** Wife	Man **vs.** Woman
Focus on God and each other	Focus on the self
Joy of giving and receiving	Unwillingness to make sacrifices
Bodies are gifts for love	Bodies are tools for use
Working together for the common good	Division and isolation
God brings us together in His image, a communion of persons.	***Satan divides and conquers to isolate us from each other.***

Based on *TOB* 28:3, 32:3 and 43:7. © Copyright 2020 by Monica Ashour. All rights reserved.

The Husband as Hero

Erin and Zack were happily married, but they knew their time was short—Zack suffered from cystic fibrosis, a terminal disease. Zack was determined to provide for his wife through the difficulties that lay ahead. Since he knew that sooner or later he would not be able to speak, he planned to speak with the language of his body: if he turned his hand over, it would mean "start praying." Several times in the hospital, Zack struggled to turn his hand over. Everyone in the room began praying. On the night of their 4th anniversary, Erin tearfully kissed Zack as he drew his last breath.

Zack's actions fulfilled these words from the Bible: "Husbands, love your wives, even as Christ loved the church and handed himself over for her" (Eph. 5:25). Each husband is meant to be a hero to his wife, which often entails suffering and self-sacrifice. He is constantly called to purify his heart of selfish motives so that he can love his wife well. The heroic task of a husband is to be **for** his wife. He is to know and protect her heart. All humans long to be fully known; a husband enters into the mystery of his wife's heart by knowing her hopes and dreams, her joys and pains, her preferences and fears. These require his daily time and attention. All heroic husbands want their wives not just to survive, but to thrive. A holy husband receives strength from God to keep his wife and himself on the path to Heaven.

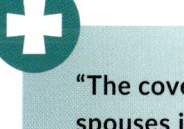

"The covenant between the spouses is integrated into God's covenant with man: 'Authentic married love is caught up into divine love.'" CCC 1639

Zack and Erin Barcevac

The Mother as Heroine

While six children were playing plastic ball in their backyard, their mom took her turn and launched the ball over the fence, hitting a homerun! Her kids cheered. As a stay-at-home mom, she taught her kids to walk, talk, sing, think, and play. Most importantly, she taught them how to stay close to Jesus and His Church. Years later, these six children are adults with successful careers and growing families of their own. They are all still very close, connected by their mother's love and by their Catholic Faith.

What does a heroic mother do? She gives life to her children with her time, attention, love, and her very body as she bears them for nine months. From conception to adulthood, children are formed by their mothers, whose bodily presence communicates, "I am **for** you." A mom makes a house a home.

Who knows your favorite ice cream flavor or stuffed animal and keeps track of your allergies? Who was with you during a surgery? Who knows your gifts, struggles, and heartaches? Mom. She makes an impact on the world by forming you to be a heroic adult. Good mothers imitate Mother Mary, the archetype of all motherhood.

"She opens her mouth in wisdom; kindly instruction is on her tongue…. Her children rise up and call her blessed…."

Prv. 31:26–28

The Father as Hero

St. Joseph was the husband of Mary and foster-father of Jesus. Humble, heroic, and holy, he recognized the voice of God and acted upon it. He led his family away from King Herod's wrath into Egypt in order to keep them safe. St. Joseph provided for his family as a carpenter, teaching Jesus the value of noble, disciplined, and hard work. A strong man of faith, St. Joseph has been given the title "Protector of the Church."

What does a heroic father do? He helps bring children into the world and then takes responsibility for them. He sets an example of integrity and courage for his sons and daughters. Dads develop the wisdom to know when to listen, scold, hug, joke, advise, or challenge their children. No wonder we call priests *Father*, for they are called to care for their flocks in a similar way.

Consider the immense responsibility that God gave to fathers, for they bear His own title, Father. In fact, our image of God is often based on our earthly fathers, for good or for ill. Great dads spend time in prayer to know and imitate God. Just like God the Father, emotionally connected fathers form secure, loving children. Good fathers imitate God the Father, the archetype of all fatherhood.

"As a father has compassion on his children, so the LORD has compassion on those who fear him." *Ps. 103:13*

Heroism: The Hard-Fought Daily Decisions

HONOR
INTEGRITY
CONCERN FOR COMMON GOOD
EXCELLENCE
DISCIPLINE
COURAGE IN SUFFERING
SEEKING WISDOM

Virtues are powerful weapons. Arm yourself with as many as you can to fight off the vices that assail you on your quest toward heroism.

COWARDICE   LYING   SELFISHNESS   DOING THE MINIMUM   LAZINESS   BULLYING   SHOWING OFF

"The body in its masculinity and femininity has been called... to become a manifestation of the [human] spirit...permeated by the Spirit of God...." *Theology of the Body 45:2; 51:6*

34

Heroic Men and Women of God

Gentlemen, how will you live out your masculinity? Will you be bold and courageous like the brothers St. Peter and St. Andrew, who left everything to follow Christ? Will you be joyful like St. John Bosco, who evangelized youth with juggling and magic tricks? Will you be like St. Thomas Aquinas, who pondered and explained the mysteries of God? Will you be a father like St. Thomas More, who led by his example of manliness and courage, even to the point of death for refusing to compromise his faith?

Ladies, how will you live out your femininity? Will you be a faithful sister like St. Scholastica, who reminded her twin brother, St. Benedict, of the primacy of love? Will you be strong like St. Catherine of Siena, who counseled the pope of her time? Will you be like St. Thérèse of Lisieux, who, though a cloistered sister, changed the world through her deep insights into the Faith? Will you be a mother like St. Monica, who prayed diligently for those closest to her?

By living virtuously, you become a great-souled person, a real hero or heroine who chooses the way of self-gift and courageous love for others.

Points to Ponder:
1. Who are the best moms you have known, and who are the best dads you have known? How do they display heroic qualities?
2. Which family archetype can you relate to best and why? Which story struck you the most?

Mission: Write a letter to your dad, older brother, or father figure. Describe how you see him as a hero. Write another letter to your mom, older sister, or mother figure. Tell her the ways you see her as a heroine.

4 Attraction and Love

Falling in Love... With Pizza?

What are the things you love? How many of you **love** pizza? Do you **adore** chocolate? Are you **crazy about** soccer? Do you **idolize** the music of your favorite band? Notice that when people feel passionate about "things," they sometimes use romantic language.

Truthfully, we experience all kinds of attractions. We are attracted to a certain sports team, a preferred brand of clothes, or a favorite music group. Something about them pulls us in; something about them makes us happy. Attraction, simply put, is to experience something as good, true, or beautiful and to be drawn to it.

Even though we express different degrees and types of love, we only have one word for it in English. We can say, "I love pizza" and "I love my grandma" in the same breath.

The ancient Greeks, however, recognized there were different kinds of love and developed different names for each one—*storge*, *philia*, *eros*, and *agape*.

"The more a person loves, the more he resembles God."
YOUCAT 402

36

Types of Love

Greek	Meaning	Theology of the Body Meaning
Storge	Family love	Love within the family, teaches love and acceptance of self and others
Philia	Friendship love	Love between peers, focuses on companionship and common interests
Eros	Romantic love	Love that desires union with the beloved through a total gift of self
Agape	Self-sacrificial love	Love purely interested in what's best for the other

© Copyright 2020 by Monica Ashour. All rights reserved.

Speaking of Love

The Greeks understood there are various movements of the heart for different kinds of relationships and that each has a proper place in our lives. We live in a world that tends to overemphasize romantic love (*eros*) at the expense of the other three. But human persons are meant to experience different types of loves. When we are aware of these four kinds of love, we can better understand attraction and decipher our feelings.

The Hierarchy of Loves

St. Augustine instructed people to put their loves in the right order. He warned against the danger of placing something or someone above love for God. You might love chocolate, but chocolate cannot save you! When you put God first, your love for family, friends, pets, sports, and even chocolate, will fall into the right place. God is not in competition with other loves. After all, He made them. Loving God as the Source of all Good leads us to properly enjoy all creation.

The Heart of Attraction

When you experience feelings of attraction, you should discern what to do about them—which may be to do nothing. Being attracted to or impressed by others is a universal experience. Do not be fooled by our culture that says every feeling of attraction is romantic. It is normal to delight in friends, whether they are our own sex or the other sex. You are capable of self-mastery, which is the ability to say "no" to acting on feelings alone, as well as "yes" to respecting others and yourself.

Attraction comes from admiration. We are naturally drawn to people who are good-looking or talented—maybe you know a boy who can play the piano well, or throw a football really far.

Maybe you have met a girl who has a contagious smile, or who leads her volleyball team to victory with her powerful serve. It is good to admire these things. In fact, attraction often starts with noticing something through the senses—a person has great hair, strong muscles, or a charming personality.

Attraction is also often accompanied by feelings of excitement—both physical and emotional. Your heart starts beating faster, or you feel butterflies in your stomach. Through these signals, your body is speaking a language: *I am so happy to be around this person*. This is a natural response. But attraction is not always meant to lead to romance, and in fact, admiration can be the basis of a strong friendship. Stay grounded in *philia* (friendship love), and give your connections with various people time to grow.

Because of their differences, men and women naturally experience romantic attraction to each other (*eros*). This is part of God's wise and beautiful plan so that they eventually fall in love, get married, and start a family. For now, romantic attraction can wait, and in the meantime, you can practice self-mastery, self-respect, and non-exclusive friendships.

😭 Help! I Think I'm in Love! 😍

Why do I feel butterflies in my stomach?

Why do I keep feeling embarrassed?

Why am I suddenly speechless?

What do I do?!

Ask everyone for advice!

Keep all my feelings to myself!

Everyone tells me to follow my heart.

Daydream all day about my crush.

It's too scary! Crawl under a rock!

Be alone forever under my rock.

Obsess and make a plan to attract the person I like.

Mission accomplished! We're a couple, but...

Why do I feel so jealous?

Why do I feel so insecure?

Why do I never see my friends anymore?

Talk to a trusted adult or friend!

Think carefully.

AND

Talk to God.

Am I ready for dating?

YES — NO

Am I ready for marriage? — NO → Channel my feelings in healthy ways.

Have fun with friends and family.

Learn and be involved at school.

Develop lots of friendships.

Spend time in prayer with God.

Loving all people as brothers and sisters allows self-knowledge for happy, secure relationships.

Going too far, too fast, leads to hurt & heartbreak. ⟶ But there is hope

© Copyright 2018 by Monica Ashour. All rights reserved.

Training the Heart

At your age, you are growing and maturing into young adults, and members of the other sex suddenly start to seem a little more interesting. However, it is important to recognize that maturing is a process. Right now, your heart is in training. You might even say you are training your future self for real love.

The gift of *eros* helps us discover real love. There is a purpose to romantic love; we are not meant to date aimlessly. *Eros* is meant to propel a man and woman to give themselves to each other as husband and wife. Someday you will be ready to say "I do," but for now, the best thing you can do is to grow in virtue, so when the time is right, you can find real and lasting love.

Imagine a woman who signs up now for a marathon twelve months away. She's not ready to run 26.2 miles today. Luckily, the race is a long way off, so what should she do until then? Should she distract herself, ignoring her workouts, and hope for the best? No! She should start training now so that when race-day arrives, she is ready—otherwise she is likely not to finish.

Now, imagine a young man who joins the military. Would he be given a uniform and a few supplies and immediately be sent to the front lines? Of course not! He must endure intense drills and preparation so that when he gets to the battlefield, he knows what to do. In light of this, how can you prepare to become a good future spouse? What are some practical steps to take? Take a look at the chart on the next page.

Training for Real Love

Do	Don't
Enjoy lots of different kinds of friendships.	Worry or focus on finding "the one."
Enjoy group activities.	Date someone seriously when you are too young.
Put your talents and gifts into action.	Isolate yourself with excessive entertainment.
Learn from the men and women you admire in your life.	Choose poor role models or imitate celebrities with low moral standards.
Grow in your relationship with Jesus, especially at Mass.	Ignore Christ's presence at Mass or mechanically go through the motions.

© Copyright 2018 by Monica Ashour. All rights reserved.

"Do you not know that the runners in the stadium all run in the race, but only one wins the prize? Run so as to win. Every athlete exercises discipline in every way. They do it to win a perishable crown, but we an imperishable one." 1 Cor. 9:24–25

Love Persons, Use Things

One of the best ways to work on loving as God loves is to learn the proper way to respond to people versus things. For example, you use a laptop to do your homework because it is a thing. Like all matter, it is a gift that can be enjoyed for a good purpose. We can appreciate the intricate technological design of a computer that performs many functions.

However, people are not to be used like computers, since they are more than mere matter. Each person is a son or daughter of God the Father. EveryBODY is a mystery, with visible and invisible characteristics. This means the only proper response to a person is love, which requires willing the good of each and every person. Especially in the area of attraction, always remember that the opposite of love is use.

How Do You Approach Persons and Things?

Persons	Things
Are to be loved	May be used
Are not to be controlled	Can be controlled
Are subjects of their own lives	Can be objectified
Make their own choices	Have no choice
Are free	Have no freedom
Are mysterious	Are predictable

© Copyright 2018 by Monica Ashour. All rights reserved.

Seeing the Whole Person

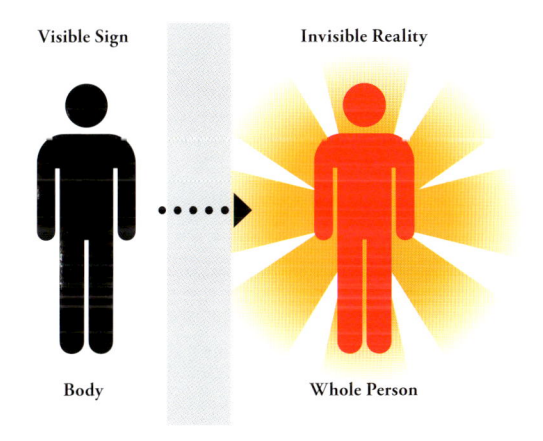

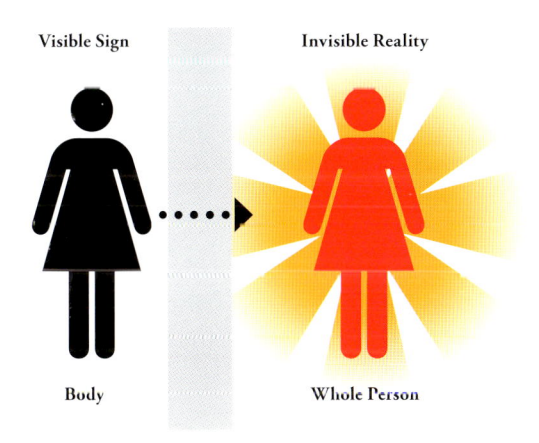

Visible Sign — Body
Invisible Reality — Whole Person

Visible Sign — Body
Invisible Reality — Whole Person

Based on *TOB* 12:4-13:1; 14:2-4. © Copyright 2018 by Monica Ashour. All rights reserved.

When attraction occurs, we can be reminded that everyBODY is a gift to be treasured. When you like a dessert for its taste and a sport for its excitement, you use them for mere enjoyment. But when you like a boy for his humor, or a girl for her kindness, they deserve more. Desserts and sports are objects to be used; persons are to be reverenced. **Use** puts the focus on one's own enjoyment; **love** appreciates a person as a gift for his or her own sake.

The Body and Identity

When we see the human body not as mere matter, but as a visible sign of the whole person, we have developed a sacramental vision. We **are** our bodies, and so much more. Do you strive to see yourself and others as persons with the fullness of sacramental sight?

Train your eye, mind, and heart to see the body as a sacrament—as a visible sign of each person, who is a gift, deserving love. This lays a good foundation for identity. A boy can say, "I am my body," since his body reveals that he is a gift, a human person, a male, and deserving love. A girl can say, "I am my body," since her body reveals that she is a gift, a human person, a female, and deserving love. Identity is based on the truth found in God's design of the human person made male or female and on the truth that each person is a gift, loved eternally by the Father.

Do Not Awaken Love... Yet

In the *Song of Songs* from the Old Testament, the young maiden tells her friends: "Do not arouse or awaken love before love's time" (see Song of Songs 2:7, 3:5, 8:4). In other words, to act upon attraction immediately or impulsively is like pulling apart the petals from a rose that has just begun to bloom. Be patient and real love will come along when the time is right.

To the Boys:

You are typically more visually motivated than girls. The female body is attractive, but you have a duty to protect girls from being used. So, what do you do? First, you can thank God for the beauty you see in girls. Be careful not to entertain thoughts beyond that. Girls are your sisters in Christ. Be strong and turn away from images that turn women and their bodies into objects. The language of your male body is strength. Who is more heroic—the boy who gives into temptation and uses a girl, or the boy who resists temptation and honors her?

To the Girls:

You typically feel emotions more readily than boys do. Remember you are in charge of your heart. Train yourself to be modest in word, dress, and action. Boys are your brothers in Christ. The language of your female body is beauty which naturally attracts. Who is more heroic—the girl who draws too much focus upon herself, hoping to win attention and approval, or the girl who protects her dignity by discerning the proper time, place, and way to express herself?

"Christ...assigns the dignity of every woman as a task to every man... also the dignity of every man to every woman."

Theology of the Body 100:6

Bodily Presence Is a Present

At your age, it is important to develop lots of solid friendships. As you do so, keep in mind that the body matters. If you spend all of your time on social media or use it as a substitute for life, you miss out on being bodily present with others. Remember, your bodily presence is a present.

Theresa had a terrible day at school and needs someone to confide in. If she posts about it online, she may get a flurry of sympathetic emojis, but is that what she needs? If she sits down with her friend Christie, what happens? Christie nods her head, cries in sympathy, or hugs her warmly—all of these bodily actions express the language of friendship more deeply than any online comment can.

Miguel stays up late every night to play video games. When he gets home from school, all he wants to do is shut his door so he can explore a virtual reality. He knows he could hang out and shoot hoops with his friend AJ, but video games are an easier choice. One afternoon, Miguel decides instead to play basketball with AJ and is surprised to discover how this physical activity and friendship offer him greater fulfillment.

You were made for more! You were made to live your embodied masculinity or femininity in a way that changes the world. Let's look at the Man and the woman whose lives changed history more than any other—Jesus and Mary.

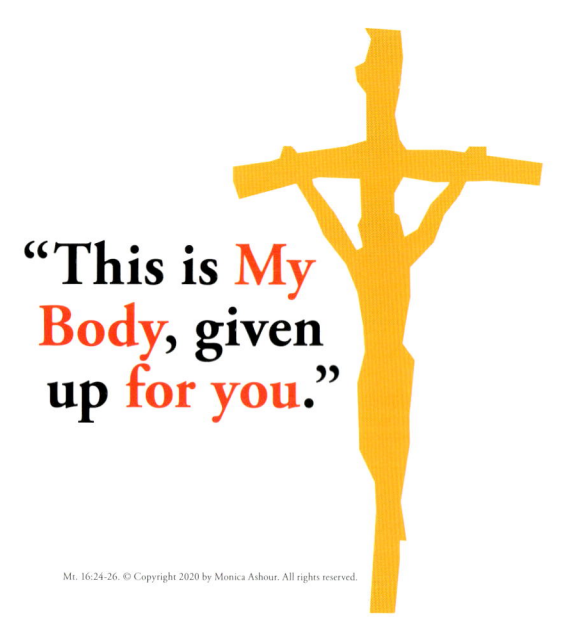

"This is **My Body**, given up **for you**."

Mt. 16:24-26. © Copyright 2020 by Monica Ashour. All rights reserved.

Behold the Man!

Every time we see a crucifix, we are reminded that Jesus heroically gave His Gift of Self by laying down His very life. As the archetype of masculinity, Our Lord provides an example for all of us to imitate. He defeated the enemy of mankind—Satan—by giving up His very Body so that each one of us might be saved. What immense strength of resolve it takes to live and die for others! It is the hallmark of a heroic man.

Does Jesus **protect**? He protected us from being enslaved to sin and its consequence: Hell. Does He **connect**? Profoundly. The Son of God became human and lived among us. He gives us divine life to connect us to God and others eternally in Heaven. Jesus said, "…I go and prepare a place for you" (Jn. 14:3). Jesus embraced His humanity and His masculinity wholeheartedly. They became the path to our salvation.

> "Jesus knew and loved us each and all during his life, his agony, and his Passion, and gave himself up for each one of us.…" *CCC 478*

> "My soul proclaims the greatness of the Lord; my spirit rejoices in God my Savior. For he has looked upon his handmaid's lowliness."
>
> Lk. 1:46–48

Behold Your Mother!

Jesus' mother, Mary, is the archetype of heroic femininity, for at every moment of her life, she gave the gift of self. Her example calls all of us to greatness. Just like Mary at the Annunciation, we too can boldly say "yes" to God at every moment. Even though Mary experienced tremendous suffering at the foot of the cross, her heroism remained steadfast. That is where she received her mission to be a mother to us all (see Jn. 19:26–27), when Jesus said, "Woman, behold your son," referring to John, the beloved disciple, who represents all of us. Jesus thus entrusts all of humanity to Mary's maternal care.

How does Mary **connect**? Through her Son, she can see and know each of us, her children, personally. As a tender, loving mother, she goes to God with our concrete needs. How does Mary **protect**? She, like Mother Church, wraps her mantle around us, keeping evil at bay. If we are willing to cooperate, she intercedes so that God's will is done in our lives, and she protects us from sinful and self-absorbed ways. Mary embraced her femininity wholeheartedly and placed it at God's service to open the way to our salvation.

"Human life is by its nature 'co-educational' and its dignity as well as its balance depend... on 'who' she shall be for him and he for her." *Theology of the Body 43:7*

For Eternity: Boys As Male; Girls As Female

Masculinity or femininity, lived out through the uniqueness of each person, is each a mysterious sign of God's desire for union and communion for us now and for all eternity. In the face of tremendous opposition and confusion, be heroic young men and women on a quest for truth, greatness, and authentic self-giving love.

May you live the truth of your body here and now for a lifetime of confidence and peace. And, by remaining faithful to Christ, you will ultimately live the truth of your resurrected body in Heaven, when you will receive your male body or your female body back, glorified, spiritualized, and prepared for eternal joy.

Points to Ponder:
1. In the Greek list of loves (pg. 37), how does *agape* love (self-giving love) inform all the other loves?
2. Why is being bodily present to others a better choice than relating through technology? In what ways can technology lead to using people? How can it help connect people?

Mission: Make a list of things for you to do in your quest to live the gift of self heroically. Refer to pg. 41 as a guide. Come up with ways in which you can practice seeing your classmates as your brothers and sisters in Christ.